STAGECOACH DAYS

A Sunset Book

STAGECOACH DAYS

By Vickie Hunter and Elizabeth Hamma
Illustrated by Randy Steffen

LANE BOOKS
Menlo Park, California

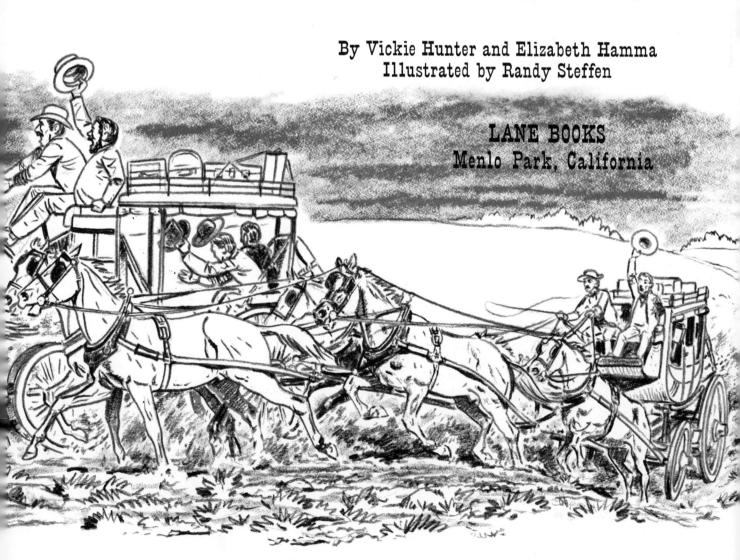

Glossary

Boot: baggage compartment at rear of coach and under driver's seat

Box: coach driver's seat

Bull-whacker: driver of ox-teams; freighter

Carry-all: light, covered carriage seating several people

Charlie: coach driver

Concord coach: stagecoach made by Abbott, Downing Co., Concord, N.H.

Corduroy road: road made of logs laid across a swamp, ribbed like corduroy cloth

Depot: railroad station

Diggings: places where gold was mined

Expressman: messenger carrying express items by whatever transportation is fastest

Groom: stableman, who takes care of horses

Hame: one of two curved bars fitted to a horsecollar, holding the traces of a harness

Hostler: stableman

Jackass: male donkey

Jehu: coach driver; from the name of a biblical character who drove fast and furiously

Leaders: horses leading a four- or six-horse team

Lines: reins

Mustang: wild horse

Reaches: bars connecting rear axles with forward part of a vehicle

Repeater: gun which fires several shots without being reloaded

Reinsman: coach driver

Ribbons: reins

Rig: harness

Road agent: highway robber

"Shotgun": stagecoach guard

Singletree: horizontal crossbar, to the ends of which the traces of a harness are attached

Stagecoach: four-wheeled, horse-drawn vehicle for passenger use. Often called a *coach* or *stage*

Stagers: men who ran the staging business

Staging: the business of carrying people and express items by stagecoach

Swing horses: horses in the center position in a six-horse team

Tapestry: heavy cloth, woven with designs and pictures, long wearing and usually expensive

Thoroughbrace: leather strap of many layers, supporting coach body

Traces: side straps by which a horse pulls a vehicle

Wheel horses: horses nearest the front of a coach

Wheelwright: a person who makes and repairs wheels

Whippletree: horizontal bar at front of coach, to which singletrees are attached

Whipster, or whip: coach driver

CONTENTS

ALL ABOARD!

Our story of western staging begins in the city of Sacramento on a hot July morning in 1849. The sun shines through the branches of the great oak trees along the river. This mid-summer day will be hot. The air is sticky and still.

This city is crowded with noisy people. Lines of sweating, excited men stand in front of all the crude tents and hastily made wooden shops. They have just one thought on their minds, *gold!* Their long journeys are almost over now. In the mountain streams near Sacramento there is gold. The stories say all a fellow has to do is pick it up. The men are buying what supplies they can find or can afford and are hurrying off to the diggings.

In the shade of an oak tree on the square, one young man quietly watches the crowds of gold seekers. He has come West to make his fortune too, and while he looks at the frantic people he is thinking of ways to do it. He has a girl back home. He promised to build a beautiful home for her and he hopes to do it with money from the gold fields of California. This

Jim Birch looked at the frantic people

young man is James E. Birch. The sun is bright and amazingly hot as Birch leaves the shady tree and goes up the street, walking slowly in the deep dust. Dust he doesn't mind. But one thing is sure; standing in cold mountain streams with these mad mobs of gold seekers is not for him.

Eating dust was part of Birch's life. Before coming West, he and his pal, Frank Stevens, had driven stage back in Providence, Rhode Island. Birch liked the feel of the ribbons in his hands and the touch of the brake to his foot. He thrilled at the sight and sound of the gallant six horses pounding ahead of him as he sat on the box of a splendid Tall Coach. That was what he would do in California. He would drive the gold seekers to the diggings in a stage.

First he would need an office. Sam Brannan's store seemed to be the busiest place in town. This would be just right for his headquarters. Young Birch knew what he was about and an agreement was made. He rented office space in a corner of Brannan's store.

Later that summer, driving a very light, spring-less wagon pulled by four mustangs, Jim drew up in front of Brannan's store.

"All aboard!" he called. "All aboard for *Birch's Line of Stages*— through to the mines!" Jim sat proudly on the box with a bull-whacker's whip held in his hands to guide the nervous team. He sat as straight and tall as he had in the fine coaches he'd driven back East. With loud shouts and yells the men waiting in front of the store piled their gear in and crowded up behind him. Springless wagon or fancy coach, right now they didn't care. The team moved ahead, leaving clouds of dust behind. The stage was off! *Birch's Line of Stages—all aboard!*

The road led east out of Sacramento, past Sutter's Fort, and followed the south bank of the American River. It led up into the foothills of the Sierra Nevada, then dipped down into the valley where Sutter had built his sawmill. There the carpenter, James Marshall had found the precious yellow flakes of gold. The narrow pack trail to the mill was now a well beaten, wide roadway. It was crowded with travelers on foot or on horseback and with trains of pack mules and freighters' wagons. For a ride in his rickety wagon, either way, the miners gladly paid Jim thirty-two dollars, or two ounces of gold.

Business was good for the young New Englander. In September he

The team moved ahead, leaving clouds of dust

8

hired another driver, Anson Briggs, and announced that Birch's Line would now run two stages to the diggings at Coloma. He delivered express items, mail and the Sacramento papers regularly to the people along the route. This mail and express (gold to be banked, a dozen fresh eggs, or a seamstress's finished sewing) were an important part of stage service.

Heavy rains began in the fall. The once dusty roads became muddy streams. Wagons sank to their hubs and had to be unloaded and pried out, only to sink again. Birch stopped his stage service for the winter.

In the spring he would continue, but Jim Birch would not be content with springless wagons and half-wild horses. In just three years this same young driver of the rickety wagon would be the president of a staging business valued at more than a million dollars. He began with a wagon load of men on a trip that was a little more than forty miles.

Although Jim Birch was the first to offer regularly scheduled stage service in California, his wasn't the only stage service. During those first wild years of the rush for gold, other ambitious fellows hauled folks up to the diggings now and then. However, they didn't make staging a regular business. They knew very little about driving teams of mustangs in

the mountains where there often were no roads or trails at all. They didn't take the right care of their animals and couldn't keep the stages running day after day.

Down in Stockton a fellow named Alexander Todd was in the express business and—almost—in the stage business too. He rode a mule on his rounds to the camps. His "stage" was a rowboat on the San Joaquin River. He let the passengers row his little boat and only charged them $16 apiece. For a letter delivered to the mining camps from the post office in San Francisco, Todd got $4. He carried gold dust back in butter kegs for the miners and made even more profit for himself. For a few months, this pioneer mailman made as much as a thousand dollars a day.

There was another stage line that ran from San Jose to San Francisco —sometimes. John Whistman ran this public stage service. It was a nine-hour ride in the old French carryall Whistman used as a stage. Mustangs, mules, or whatever he could get, served as the team. At the end of the line the animals were turned loose to graze in the big corral. There was no schedule, and no promise when the next stage would leave.

Without the great numbers of gold seekers to demand rides, public transportation in other parts of the West developed more slowly. Farmers didn't need to travel as fast as get-rich-quick miners. Up in Oregon Territory as early as 1846, settlers had a weekly passenger service from Oregon City to the Tualatin settlement. This stage passenger service was powered by eight oxen. Service was slow, but business was good.

Hauling freight or people or gold was a good way to make a fortune in the new land, but you had to know what you were doing. As experienced stagemen began arriving in California, they too saw the need for better ways to travel. Hundreds of people were arriving every day. Hundreds more were returning from the diggings. Some were broke, sick, and discouraged, but many others were as rich as kings. Miners with leather pouches full of gold dust didn't like walking or riding a mule back to town. They didn't like the rutty roads and the slow wagons. They wanted the real stagecoach service they had been used to back home, and they were willing to pay for it.

Warren Hall and Jared "Bob" Crandall were newcomers to California too, but they were both experienced stage line owners. They bought the line that John Whistman drove to San Jose and began a regularly scheduled stagecoach service in 1850. Another stage line to San Jose (which was the capital of California then) was run by Ackley and Maurison. One day they had a race to see just who was the fastest.

That race took place when California became the 31st state of the United States in September of 1850. The news spread quickly. Soon important state officials began arriving in San Jose by stage. Both stage lines wanted the honor of driving the Governor, Peter Burnett, into the capital. The governor chose a Hall and Crandall stage. He tells about the ride in his diary:

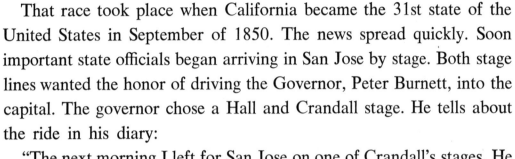

"The next morning I left for San Jose on one of Crandall's stages. He was a most excellent driver. On this occasion he drove the stage himself, and I occupied the top front seat beside him. . . . After passing over the sandy road to the mission, there was some of the most rapid driving that I ever witnessed. The distance was some fifty miles, most of the route being over smooth, dry, hard prairie. The drivers put their mustang teams to the utmost of their speed. As we flew past on our rapid course, the people flocked to the road to see what caused our fast driving and loud shouting, and without slackening our speed in the slightest degree, we took off our hats, waved them round our heads, and shouted at the tops of our voices, "California is admitted to the Union!" Upon this announcement the people along the road cheered as loudly and heartily as possible. I never witnessed a scene more exciting, and never felt more enthusiastic. I never can forget Crandall's race! He beat his competitor only a few minutes."

Another kind of race was going on in the foothills of the Sierra Nevada Mountains. Eager miners were searching for more gold. They explored the region we call the Mother Lode, and in this belt of land they found new deposits. Where the miners went, the stage would follow. Soon stage lines were spreading out from Sacramento to new mining camps. One went to Stockton every day, two others made three trips a week to Auburn and the North Fork of the American River. Another left for Deer Creek and the Yuba River, and three lines went to Marysville and other river camps. Stage service was better all the time.

Jim Birch continued to add to his line of stages. In the early spring of

1850 his first of a series of new coaches arrived in Sacramento. His two stages called for passengers at any of the hotels in Sacramento and delivered them to Hangtown, Cold Springs, Georgetown and other camps. Mr. Briggs and a new man, Mr. Cole, drove the stages while Jim looked after the growing business. He was well known for his honesty and friendliness and well liked by everyone.

When the rains came in the fall of 1851, Jim sold his stages and went back home to marry his Julia and to build her the mansion he had promised. But he wasn't gone for long. In March of 1853 he was back, bought one of the lines he had started, and Jim Birch was in business again!

By 1853 staging in California was big business. There were eleven stage lines leaving Sacramento. It had become a real transportation center. Every day thirty or more coaches and more than three hundred passengers went through the city. More than fifteen hundred head of horses were used by freighters and stage lines. Stages met the glittering steamships that chugged up the river on the overnight trip from San Francisco. They whirled the passengers off to the mines.

Wells Fargo and Company had opened its Western offices in 1852 and was becoming the outstanding express and banking business of the West.

Stages met the glittering steamships

But there was no organization to the stage lines. With the various stage lines all battling for business, the traveler got poor service.

Now Jim Birch was not only an experienced stage driver, but he was a real businessman. He knew how much money stage line owners had to spend for equipment and gear. It was expensive to bring fine coaches all the way from New Hampshire and fine stage horses were costly too. Jim talked to his friend Frank Stevens and other stage owners and on New Year's Day in 1854 the news was out! A new company had been formed. More than half of the stage lines in California had united to make one giant transportation system, *The California Stage Company*. Its officers were all staging men who knew every part of the business from the rigging of a thoroughbrace to the stocking of a line. Jim Birch and Frank Stevens, who were both just twenty-five years old, were chosen President and Vice President.

The company owned over nine hundred head of horses and over a hundred coaches. They were, at that time, the largest staging company in the world.

Express and stage business had grown slowly in southern California. In 1852 Phineas Banning had opened the first stage company in that area, and D. W. Alexander started a route between Los Angeles and San Diego. In 1853 the two ends of the state were connected by a stage route along the coast.

From the northern end of their line at Shasta City, the California Stage Company stocked a road to Yreka, using the old emigrant road. Birch was determined to put the line as far north as Portland, Oregon. To do this, the company had to fight Indians and build long stretches of road. At last, in 1860, stage and mail service between Sacramento and Portland was opened. Seven hundred and ten miles could be traveled in safety, with comfort and speed.

Along the entire route there were sixty stations, seventy-five hostlers, and thirty-five drivers. There were twenty-eight coaches, thirty stage wagons, and five hundred head of horses. It was supposed to take seven days to make this trip, but the actual time was six days and seven hours.

The quiet, handsome, brown-eyed young Easterner had made quite a change in the West. He had come to make a fortune, and he did! But money alone wasn't the important thing. He was helping to build the once sleepy West by taking people where they had to go.

Jim Birch was one of the first to bring the finest eastern coaches out west. Other lines might use any kind of cart or wagon that would hold people, but not Jim! Any kind of wagon could be used as a stage, but there was only one Tall Coach for him.

Birch's *California Stage Company* ordered fine Concord Coaches!

4- SEAT CONCORD

2- SEAT MUD WAGON

STAGES ROLLING

Clipper ships from the east coast of the United States flew over the ocean waves under great white sails and dumped heavy cargos of people and goods in San Francisco. The very first of the many stagecoaches to travel the dusty mountain and valley roads in California came west lashed to the deck of one of those clipper ships. On a June day of 1850, the first eastern-made coach rolled around the plaza in San Francisco, pulled by six splendid bay horses. Great crowds turned out just to look at it. Other wheeled vehicles were arriving every day from Australia and the Oriental countries, but it was the skillfully made eastern coaches that soon were to provide transportation for the miners and settlers of the West.

Without a doubt, the finest coach the world has ever known was the Concord Coach! Now that is quite a thing to say about a coach, but it's true. This was the coach made by Abbott-Downing Company of New Hampshire.

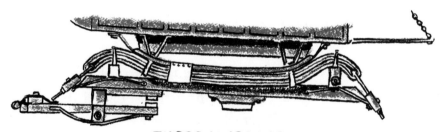

THOROUGHBRACE
SUSPENSION OF MUD WAGONS
AND CELERITY WAGON

CELERITY WAGON

MUD WAGON OR PASSENGER HACK

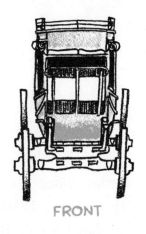

FRONT

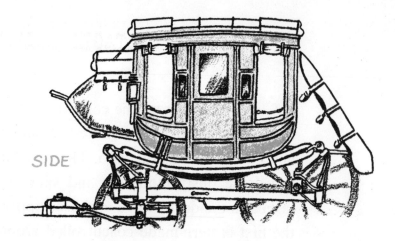

SIDE

THE CURVED CONCORD
COACH BODY

16

It was a gloriously beautiful coach to look at with bright red paint on the body, shiny black leather boots and straps, bright yellow wheels and running gear. The paint work was done with careful brush strokes and was polished as smooth as a mirror. As lovely as that may be, fine paint doesn't make a fine coach. So that isn't the only reason why stagemen all over the world wanted to own Concords. The coach was a masterpiece of workmanship throughout its construction. It was made to do a special job, and it was made to last.

On the Concord were two lengths of leather straps that supported the wooden body of the coach. Those leather straps, called thoroughbraces, were made of many layers of the thickest steer hides. They allowed the body to rock back and forth and sideways too. They did more than even

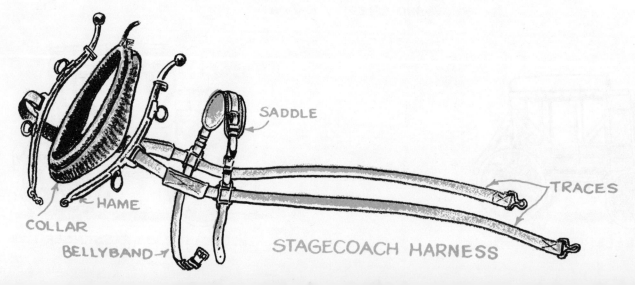

SADDLE

TRACES

HAME

COLLAR

BELLYBAND

STAGECOACH HARNESS

steel springs do today. While they did serve as springs to the body of the coach, they had the even more important job of absorbing the shocks for the team. Heavy jerks on the traces due to any rocks or ruts in the road (and there were many) were almost eliminated.

It may be a little hard to understand just how valuable those thorough-braces were, but without them there very possibly would have been no staging. Without them, any vehicle carrying the loads that had to be carried, and going as fast as stages went, would have killed or ruined the horses. Passengers could stand a little shaking up, but horses couldn't take harsh treatment and still do their work.

The wheel of the Concord was another masterpiece. Other wagon wheels would warp or shrink and go to pieces in the hot or cold climates out West, but not wheels made by Abbot-Downing Company. Each spoke was hand made and fitted and balanced to the rim and hub. This was done so carefully that your eye could scarcely find where it joined. The woods were well dried to stand heat and cold. Wheels had to stand hard treatment, for they rolled over the worst of roads.

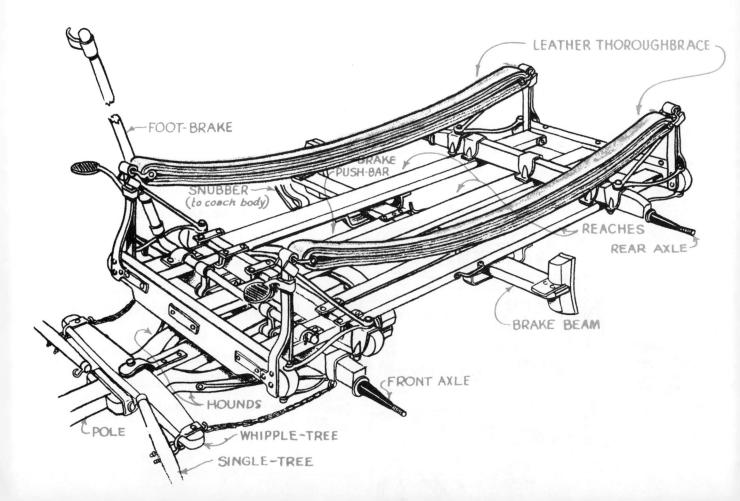

Lewis Downing had been making fine horse-drawn coaches and other vehicles since 1837. He copied the shape of the old English Coach. Then he changed and added details here and there to make it even better. As time was to prove, he made a better coach than the world had ever known. His coaches were ordered by stagemen all over the world. There were Concords traveling the roads of the eastern states, down in Mexico and South America, in South Africa and Australia.

When Downing's coach makers began there were only a few well trained workmen who used the simplest hand tools to make each wooden part of the coach the right size and shape. They had two saws, powered by horsepower. Otherwise, they had no machinery. As the business grew, they added the best equipment and machinery they could buy. Still, each coach was almost a hand-made product. Only the most skillful men made the coaches, and only the very best materials were used. These crafts-men were well paid. They were highly trained men and important citizens

If you were to divide an orange evenly, then try to fit the curved sections together again, you might understand a little better how the wooden panels for the body of the Concord were shaped. These panels were carefully curved on a form, dampened, then clamped around the edges. The coach body was rounded and curved. These wooden panels were hard to make without our modern tools. Yet the panels were more carefully joined than fine furniture is today.

The coaches were made in three sizes. They could hold six, nine, or even twelve passengers inside. The body of the coach was so strong that an additional nine or twelve passengers could ride on top. Inside, fine tapestry, embroidered cloth, or leather was used to cover and to pad the

seats and walls. This gave the passengers protection against the bumps of the road, and was nice to look at. Western coaches had to stand very rough treatment, so leather was used often. There were about fifteen inches of space inside to seat each person. (You can imagine this would be a tight squeeze, especially when ladies in their full skirts were passengers.)

It took the better part of twelve to fourteen ox hides to make the leather boots and thoroughbraces. The leather boots in the front and back of the body held the cargo—mail bags, express boxes, round-topped trunks and miners' packs. Sometimes, even, a passenger would crawl into the boot and curl up for a nap.

The wonderful Concord Coach wasn't the only coach made by Abbot-Downing Company. They also made a coach called a Hack Wagon or California Mud Wagon. They were used in place of the Concords when the roads were muddy. The Concord, you must understand, was a heavy vehicle. The mud wagon, true to its name, could go many places where the Concord couldn't because it was lighter.

There were probably many more mud wagons out West than Concords. It cost quite a bit of money (about fifteen hundred dollars) to buy a Concord. In those early staging days many companies just couldn't afford to buy magnificent coaches. They bought the cheaper mud wagons for about five hundred dollars. Now these operated on leather thorough-braces too, but they didn't give the passengers as nice a ride. The body of the mud wagon was square like a box. It was placed on rounded irons which were shaped like the rounded, bottom part of the Concord. Then, these irons rested on the thoroughbraces. This was an easier, cheaper way of giving the teams and passengers some of the benefits of the thoroughbrace.

Mud wagons or Concords, stagecoaches came in many different styles and shapes. There were other coach makers in the East besides Abbot-Downing, too. Most of them copied Downing's thoroughbrace, though few if any of them took the time to make a coach as carefully.

After a few years or months of digging gold, many Westerners saw that it wasn't so much fun after all. Some of these disappointed miners had been wheelwrights, blacksmiths, wagon and coach makers in the East. They decided to get rich by working at their former trades out West, so they began ordering fine eastern woods and wagon parts. The wood had to be shipped around Cape Horn. They began building their own shops and factories. Usually they continued to use eastern wood, for it was harder and better for the body of the wagons and the wheels.

Now another new industry began to grow, for wherever people were moving, blacksmiths were needed. They built many of the vehicles needed out West. Often they ordered spare parts for repairing coaches. Sometimes they even assembled these parts into usable wagons. Some men who began small blacksmith shops found themselves gradually doing more carriage making than anything else.

Sacramento and Stockton were carriage-making centers in California. Seattle, Portland, and Tacoma were busy repairing the coaches that rattled over the corduroy roads in Washington and Oregon. Practically every good-sized town in the West could claim a blacksmith and a wagon maker by 1865. Usually these wagon makers were very proud of their

It is the Concord we think of when we hear the word "stagecoach"

work. They had small brass name plates stamped with their name and town, and they put these plates on their best wagons and coaches.

Many wheeled vehicles helped settle the West. Before the gold rush, Mexican ox carts were used in California. Up in Oregon Territory there were heavy freighting wagons to carry settlers' supplies from the coast steamers to their new homes. Mormon pioneers used heavy, awkward wagons and light wheelbarrows and hand carts as they crossed the Great Plains to settle in what we call Utah today. Other settlers crossed in Conestoga or simple covered wagons. Traders on the Santa Fe Trail used freight wagons pulled by ox and mule teams. But it was the stagecoach, be it a beautiful, well made Concord or light mud wagon, that made life in the West more pleasant for the settlers.

It is the Concord Coach that we think of when we hear the word "Stagecoach." Among all the many other kinds of stages, the Concord stands out as the piece of workmanship unmatched until that new invention called "the automobile" took its place.

Unless you can actually see one of those marvelous coaches today, you still might not appreciate how grand they were. Maybe this story will

help. One Concord Coach was shipped to California tied to the deck of a fast sailing ship. Around the tip of Cape Horn, storms and fierce gales hit the ship again and again. In the worst of the storms, the ship, cargo, and coach sank close to shore. They lay in the ocean for three months. Now in those months, metal began to corrode and rust in the salty water. Wooden objects were beaten against the rocks and sand by waves along the shore. Sea worms began their work. After three months in the water, the ship was raised for salvage. That Concord Coach was still in such good condition that it was put into service and was used for over fifty years! It was a truly wonderful Concord Coach.

After three months they pulled it up

THE WHIP

"Just imagine yourself," a traveler wrote in the 1850s, "seated in front of the stage, by the side of a gallant old whipster, who knows every foot of the way. Holding the lines with a firm hand and peering ahead, he cracks the whip. Away go the horses with great speed, six magnificent chestnuts with flowing manes and tails. The stillness of the night is broken by their measured tread and the rattle of the wheels over the rocks and gravel. Down and still down we plunge into the gloomy depths of the canyon. The ghostly forms of trees loom up on our left. To the right, rising far beyond . . . the towering heights of the Sierra Nevada . . . and ahead of us, darkness.

"And you, my good friend, crossing the Sierra of California once or twice in a lifetime, imagine you have done great things. You boast of

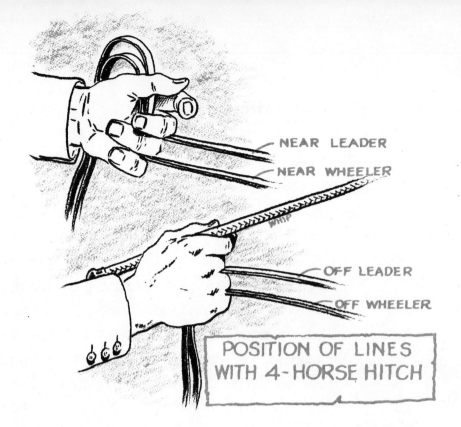

NEAR LEADER

NEAR WHEELER

OFF LEADER

OFF WHEELER

POSITION OF LINES
WITH 4-HORSE HITCH

your qualities as a traveler; you have bravely endured the cold night air, have scarcely shuddered at the narrow bridges or winced at the fearful precipices! But think of that driver! He has crossed the mountains a thousand times. He has crossed when the roads were at their worst; by night and by day, in storm and gloom and darkness; through snow and sleet and rain and burning sun and dust. Back and forth he has gone with his life balanced on the temper of a horse or the strength of a coach!"

The coaches they drove were magnificent, and the drivers were men to match them. Not just anybody could drive a stagecoach. It was no easy task to handle the six-horse teams over narrow trails carved into the sides of mountains, or on the bumpy corduroy roads or on the bottomless mud trails where the coach could sink hub deep. The driver had to be a man who could command instant action from the team, and they were hard to find in the west in the early days of staging.

Driving a six-horse stage was a skill in itself. The driver talked to the horses with his hands on the lines. With the lines he controlled the teams in all the dangerous places he must take them. He started controlling them before he ever climbed onto the box of the coach. Experts could tell what kind of driver a man would be by the way he got onto the box.

Before getting to his seat, the driver walked round his coach and team, quickly checking to see that everything was right. Then he drew the lines from their place, and carefully arranged them in his hand. He wanted them to have just the proper amount of slack. The lines from the wheel horses, from the swings, and from the leaders all went between certain fingers, as these drawings show. The driver then changed the lines into his other hand. He picked up the whip, and in three steps would be on his box. Once in his seat, he would look over the team and harness to see that no line or trace had a twist. From the box he could often see twists he might have missed on the ground. When all was ready he would usually speak a word or two to the passengers, telling them to sit tight. All of this preparation was important, for once under way he would have little time to make corrections he'd missed.

The western movies usually show drivers cracking whips to make their teams start, but this was seldom, if ever done. With the whip in his hand held as still as possible, the driver would quietly take the brake off, nod to the groom or hostler standing at the leaders' heads, who would step back and out of the way. The driver might say something to the team, but usually he spoke through the lines again. Merely by gently pulling them up, so as to feel the horses mouths, then loosening them, he let the team know it was time to go. Then they would be off! Cracking the whip over their heads or touching a horse gently with the whip was only to correct them when something was wrong.

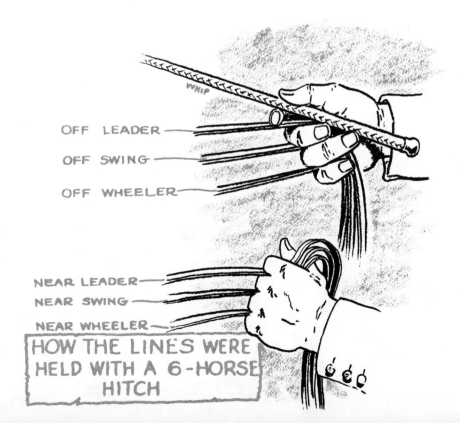

OFF LEADER

OFF SWING

OFF WHEELER

NEAR LEADER

NEAR SWING

NEAR WHEELER

HOW THE LINES WERE HELD WITH A 6-HORSE HITCH

The movie stage driver who pumps his hands and swings his body with the coach would never have been hired as a driver by men who knew how to drive. Good drivers sat straight and steady on their boxes in order to see the road. Their hands held the reins steady and firm. They did the guiding and the horses did the work.

The drivers were very proud of the harness used on their teams. They often added brass or silver ornaments or decorated the plain black leather with ivory rings. Rival drivers thought it a good joke to cut and even steal fancy rings from another driver's rig.

"The average stage driver," wrote the historian Bancroft, "was above all, lord in his way, the captain of his craft, the fear of timid passengers, the admiration of the stable boys, and the trusted agent of his employer." That kind of man was pretty hard to find.

In all the collections of stage-driver stories, from the English coachmen to the eastern drivers who froze in their seats from the cold weather,

some of the most thrilling stories are about the gallant men who drove the western stages. They were called knights of the lash, but they were known by many other names—whip, jehu, charlie. They came in many sizes and shapes, tall and lean, or short and heavy. Usually they were under forty years old, but older men drove too, and many a good whip died of a fall when his bones could no longer stand the spills.

They drove stage in all kinds of weather, on top of that open box. They were often swaggering, rough-spoken men, wearing odd styles of clothes as protection against the weather. The smart English coachmen's clothing never found its way out West. There was no special uniform for the driver. He made his own choice of clothes. Strange as it may seem, these rough fellows were usually most courteous, polite gentlemen to their passengers, especially when ladies were aboard. Certainly the finest example of staging at its best was staging in the West. In spite of all the problems facing the driver on his route—bad roads, tricky weather, strange teams, and often a wild group of passengers, he brought the coach in safe and on time.

There are many drivers we could tell you about, for western stagecoaching had its share of heroes. There was Jared "Bob" Crandall, whom we first met driving the Governor on that daring race to San Jose. Crandall heard all the talk of surveys, routes, and roads up over the Sierra beyond Placerville. Engineers and investors couldn't believe a wagon road over the Sierra was possible, but they figured it out only on paper. So one morning in June of 1857, this famous reinsman took his coach and team and drove them up into the Sierra where no team

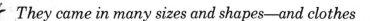

They came in many sizes and shapes—and clothes

had been before. The brave animals leaped and splashed across streams, practically climbing granite walls. Crandall had placed fresh teams at different places along the way, and finally he and coach and team sat at the summit of the Sierra. The rest of the road was almost easy, down to Cary's Mill and the Mormon Station at Genoa in what was Utah Territory then. We call it Nevada today. The settlers across the Sierra could hardly believe their eyes at the sight of Crandall's stage. Ah, he did great things, that grand reinsman! Years later, he suffered a bad fall from the box of his stage and died.

There was Jim Miller, that marvelous whip, who loved fancy clothes. He drove from Virginia City to Austin, Nevada, wearing a yellow overcoat, and yellow pants. His shoes were high-heeled, although he was over six feet tall without them. He wore a red vest and carried a huge watch that he attached to his pocket with an equally huge silver chain.

Ben Wing, who drove the Overland stage between Virginia City and Salt Lake, once had on board two deputy sheriffs and a captured horse thief. The prisoner tried to escape and was promptly shot by the deputies, who then called for a shovel. Ben didn't agree with the officers, insisting that his orders called for the body to be delivered in Salt Lake. "He's express matter, and I'm going to take him." In spite of the deputies' arguments, Ben won. The body was strapped carefully to the rear boot, went on to Salt Lake and whirled up in front of the express office with a group of whooping town boys and men behind.

Curly Bill, another mighty driver, once pulled an army officer out of his stage for insulting a lady. While pulling, Curly accidentally brought the door frame of the coach out with him.

Perhaps the best known of all was Hank Monk. His story would fill a book. Among other things, Hank was famous for his driving skill, and it was said that he could turn a six-horse coach in the middle of a street with the team at a full run, and with every line loose. The coach always stopped exactly where the most careful driver would bring it. Other drivers watching him said his skill was luck. It wasn't luck at all! Hank Monk was one of the finest of drivers. He carefully figured every turn of his hand and talked to the team with the lines in words only they could understand.

There were others, more than we could even name here. Drivers like A. D. Sterling, Reason McConnell, Cherokee Bill, Billy Hamilton, and of course, Charlie Parkhurst. Good men they were, those jehus, all of them. That is, all of them but Charlie Parkhurst.

When Jim Birch had his California Stage Lines well under way, he sent back East for his old friend, a well known eastern driver named Charlie Parkhurst. Out West, Charlie's reputation grew even more. Charlie was known as a skillful hand with the lines, and as a brave, cool-headed driver. There is the story of the time Charlie was driving across a bridge and felt it begin to shiver and go down. Charlie laid the whip to the horses like an old freight driver, and the startled team leaped as they had never leaped before. Just in time too, for the horses, coach and the passengers made the other shore to see the bridge go crashing down behind them.

Twice Charlie was held up by highwaymen. The first time Charlie threw down the box, for the robber knew this jehu carried no gun. The next time was a different story. A whole gang of road agents stopped the stage, but that made no difference to Charlie. The stage would not be stopped a second time, by one or many. This time Charlie was ready,

LIGHT HOTEL COACH

and fired a shotgun point blank at the chest of the gang leader, whipped the horses and was out of sight around the next bend before the gang realized what happened. The sheriff found the dead robber's body near the scene of the holdup attempt. After that, highwaymen left Charlie Parkhurst alone.

Charlie drove stage for nearly twenty years in California and was counted as one of the finest whips in the entire gold region, if not in the western states. After reaching the age of sixty, old Charlie decided to quit the road. Staging was a hard life and Charlie's hands could no longer hold the lines as before. In 1879 on a ranch above Watsonville, California, Charlie died, alone in a cabin. Then they learned Charlie's secret, a secret kept so carefully for over fifty years. Charlie Parkhurst, one of the finest whips in the West, was a woman!

Charlie fired point blank at the gang leader

GOLD, GUNS, AND HORSEPOWER

When large shipments of gold were being moved by stage, shotgun messengers or guards rode along with the driver. These men were often just called "shotguns." They earned their name by the guns they carried. They rode on the seat with the driver or inside the coach and protected treasures the stage was carrying. Their guns changed the minds of many would-be holdup men.

The shotgun really did the job. It was generally a double-barreled, sawed-off weapon. It was the same kind of gun used by sheriffs, bartenders, or hotel keepers who had to handle mobs. Guards and drivers needed a gun that would injure as many of a gang as possible with one shot at close range. The barrel was cut shorter so the gun would be easier to handle. Road agents or robbers usually tried to waylay the stage at places where the driver would be busy. Steep mountain trails or narrow curves were good robbery spots. Highwaymen would suddenly appear very close to the team and stage. The guard had to have his weapon ready quickly.

You must remember that although the West in those years was not as bad as it is pictured for you in the movies, it was still a booming, lusty, lawless place. By the end of 1849 California's population had grown by one hundred thousand people, and that was just the first year of the rush for gold. Not all newcomers expected to dig their gold from the mountain streams. Not all of them were honest, hard-working people. Many of them found easier ways to make their fortunes.

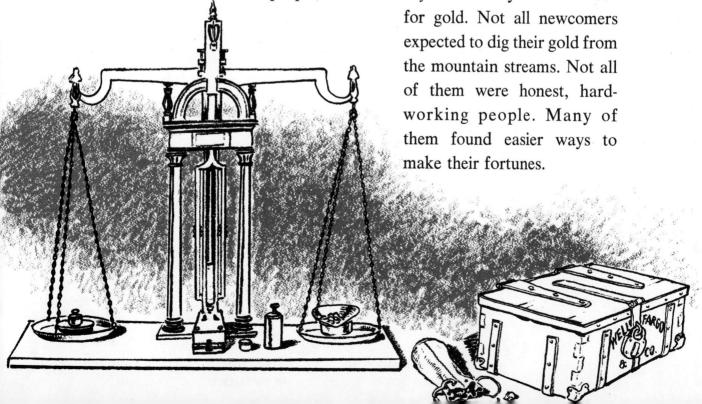

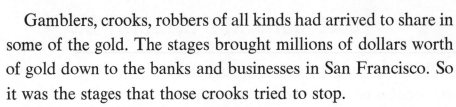

PHILADELPHIA DERINGER

32

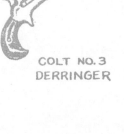

COLT NO. 3 DERRINGER

SOUTHERNER DERRINGER

SHARPS FOUR-BARREL

REMINGTON DERRINGER

Gamblers, crooks, robbers of all kinds had arrived to share in some of the gold. The stages brought millions of dollars worth of gold down to the banks and businesses in San Francisco. So it was the stages that those crooks tried to stop.

Wells, Fargo & Company, Adams & Company and other express firms had wood or metal boxes called express boxes that rode the stages of many western stage lines. In these treasure boxes were small leather pouches of the miners' gold, gold bricks called "bullion," tin boxes of gold dust, and notes like our paper money today. Each box was locked and each lock was numbered. Even the keys were numbered.

Every make, model and type of gun known in the new world guarded this gold. The beginning of western staging came at the same time as many new inventions in firearms. Old singleshot guns were being replaced with new repeaters.

The smiths and dealers who came West were men who enjoyed the fine mechanical work of making guns. In the West they found a ready market for the products they made or sold. Suddenly rich miners found it wise to protect themselves from the kind of trouble that a newly rich and lonely miner could get into. Gamblers, dancing girls and others felt the same way.

The gun they found most effective for close shooting, and the one most advertised, was the derringer. This small, large-bore, hand gun was named for a Philadelphia gun smith, Henry Derringer, Jr. It was the kind of gun that ladies could easily hide, and that men could tuck into a belt or boot top. Derringers sold for as little as $5.50 a pair. Stage drivers, guards and messengers found them useful as extra guns.

ENGLISH PEPPERBOX

SPRAGUE & MARSTON PEPPERBOX

DARLING PEPPERBOX

MOORE DERRINGER

The most popular side arm carried by Westerners was Colt's Pocket Revolver. In the 1850s this gun was a fairly new invention, but it had already become well known and almost a necessity. It could fire several times before having to be reloaded. A miner often carried one for protection. Stage drivers, messengers and guards needed guns. It wasn't unusual for a stage guard to carry a pair of revolvers, a shotgun, and even a couple of derringers tucked into his belt.

Stage drivers had their choice of guns. Wells, Fargo & Company bought many Colt Revolvers for their messengers. For this reason, these Colts are known today as the Wells, Fargo Model. After the Civil War a heavier Colt Army Revolver was carried by many guards and drivers. Many guards were so well known for their skill that holdup men stayed away.

There have probably been many more stage robberies on TV and in the movies than there ever were in all the "Wild West!" A robber had to be pretty desperate or pretty foolish before he would face a well-armed guard, driver, and a load of passengers carrying guns.

Wells, Fargo & Company's special detectives Hume and Thacker made an accurate record of their company's business for the fourteen years from 1870 through 1884. The detectives reported 313 robberies or attempted robberies of the Wells, Fargo express boxes in those fourteen years. Five men were killed while attempting to rob the stage, 11 others were killed resisting arrest, 7 were hanged by angry citizens, and 206 were sent to jail. A little arithmetic leaves us with 84 robberies apparently unpunished. But Black Bart, for example, committed over 28 robberies yet only went to jail for one. Other crooks may have committed more than one robbery, too.

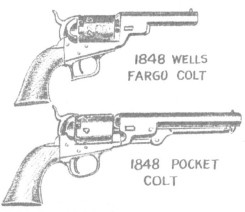

10 GAUGE
SAWED-OFF
SHOTGUN

1848 WELLS
FARGO COLT

1848 POCKET
COLT

1851 NAVY COLT

1860 ARMY COLT

1858 REMINGTON ARMY

Some of the Wells, Fargo posters offered rewards of $250 or $500 when only $150 or $300 had been stolen. Hume and Thacker's report shows that Wells, Fargo spent almost as much money protecting their cargoes as they lost in all the stage robberies. This was because the express companies, sheriffs, and citizens wanted to discourage all holdups!

In those fourteen years Wells, Fargo had seven horses killed, and thirteen stolen from the teams during robberies. This gives us an idea how important the teams were. In the early days, mustangs from the Central Valley of California were about the best animals that could be found. Travelers in those days told of seeing great herds, numbering as many as fifteen thousand. Some larger-sized Spanish horses from the ranchos joined these wild herds. Eventually they produced a stronger, but still wild animal often called the "California Horse." They were between fourteen and fifteen hands high and weighed from nine hundred to twelve hundred pounds. At the Horse Markets in Sacramento and San Francisco they sold for $75 to $150.

Some stage horses were just "horses," but many stagemen began importing better animals as soon as they began buying better coaches. They needed strong coach teams to pull the Concord, which weighed twenty-five hundred pounds unloaded. Owners and drivers liked to see the beautiful animals moving smoothly ahead of the coach, and passengers liked to say they rode in the best outfit on the road.

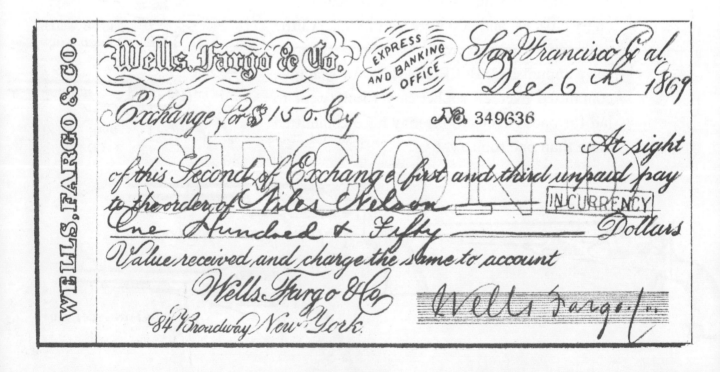

In 1851 some heavy-work animals were brought from Australia. Other teams were coming around the Horn on sailing ships from the eastern and southern states. Horses and mules were driven overland in large remudas, or herds. Others came with the wagon trains of settlers.

The very finest stagecoach horses were called "American horses" or "Trotters." Although they were only a little taller and a few hundred pounds heavier than the California horses, they had been specially bred for their work and were muscled in all the right places. The very best of these animals sold for $1000 to $1500 each. Some well matched, well trained pairs were said to have sold for as much as $4000.

The horses were valued for their speed, as well. A good running horse with a light man on his back will run a mile in less than two minutes.

Millions in gold passed through Wells, Fargo offices

Trotters that took three minutes to go a mile were about the "slowest horses worth driving." Pulling a loaded coach over the best roads, a really fast team might average as much as fifteen miles an hour. It's hard to say just how fast stage teams in the West traveled, because their times and speeds changed with the roads, weather, and other conditions. They averaged better than ten miles an hour, so you know they were really moving.

A well trained team knew how to work together; their hooves even hit the ground at the same time. They had matched gaits, that is, their right front legs moved together, and their left rear legs. The better trained the horse was, of course, the more he was worth. The animals learned to turn with the touch of the rein, to stop, back up, and follow other necessary commands. Smart, light-weight horses were put in the front of the team. They were called leaders. Heavier horses able to pull more of the load took the wheel and swing (center) positions. Once they learned their job, that was where they worked on each run.

Depending on the kind of roads and the country, stage stations were from ten to twenty miles apart. At the station, the hostler or station keeper had a fresh team harnessed and ready to snap into place as soon as the coach stopped. The tired team was unhooked from the stage; they rested a day before being used again. If the company had several teams, the animals might work only one day out of three.

The animals were cared for by the hostler. He could lose his job right away if anyone ever caught him mistreating or neglecting an animal. After each run he cooled the animals off and washed them. He carefully checked their feet and legs for any sore, tender, or bruised places, and brushed them down. Then he put them in a clean stall with a quart of grain and some hay. Then he had to clean each animal's harness with saddle soap or soap and water and a brush. Sweat rotted the leather and harness was expensive. Usually each horse had his own harness fitted to him as carefully as a man's shirt collar and hung in a certain place near his stall.

You may think this was a lot of work, and it was. Without the horses or mules the stages couldn't roll. Horsepower pulled the stage that carried the men and guns that guarded the gold!

THE BAD MEN AND THE GOOD

Doctor Thomas J. Hodges was a well educated young man. He could have been a respected, successful medical man, but he died at the end of a hangman's rope. Soon after his arrival in California he began looking for easier ways to make money. This landed him in jail, but in 1856 he escaped with a few pals. Using the name of "Tom Bell," the doctor and his gang robbed lone travelers and expressmen near the mining camps.

Their most famous holdup attempt was on Sam Langton's stage in August of 1856. Bell learned through one of his gang that a certain stage had a treasure box holding $100,000 in gold. There were several passengers on the stage, the driver, John Gear, and the shotgun messenger, an experienced guard named Bill Dobson. As the stage was

Passengers joined the fight

lumbering up a steep hill close to Marysville, Bell and part of his gang appeared in the road and ordered the stage to "Halt." They were masked and armed. Guard Dobson didn't waste a minute, but began unloading his shotgun at the men, then pulled his two revolvers and kept firing. Several men passengers joined in the fight. The surprised gang fired back, but soon decided this was too much to handle and rode away.

Over forty shots had been fired. A woman passenger had been killed; driver Gear was shot in the arm, and another passenger was hit in the leg. Dobson's quick thinking and action saved the treasure, and he escaped without a scratch!

This crime against the stage was everybody's business. The best citizens around the country helped to track the crooks. The hunt lasted several months, but Tom Bell was captured. The posse gave him a few hours to write some last letters and then quickly hanged him.

We hear many stories of the "gallant holdup men," men who only turned to crime because they'd been hurt. These bold, daring fellows really didn't mean to do wrong, the stories say. They were really "nice men in their hearts." We hear tales of men like Tom Bell, who stopped to care for an injured man, shot by one of his gang. He loaded the patient on a waiting teamster's wagon, and collected his doctor's fee from the unwilling teamster. Other robbers were reported to be real gentlemen, hidden of course by the mask. They were always polite.

"Sir," says a timid victim, "you've taken my last cent."

"Ah, keep it," says the bold bandit, and to the driver of the waiting stage, he adds, "Keep yours too. I wouldn't rob a hard-working man."

If there were men like these in the West at all, they were few! Stories often grow into legends, and apparently this is what happened in the tales of the western badman. They were just that—real badmen! You didn't point a gun at another man in those days just for fun. If you carried a weapon at all, you were expected to know how to use it. Those robbers did.

There were men like Tiburcio Vasquez, called the meanest brute ever

The "shotgun" knew how to use his weapon

to use a gun. There was "Red-handed Dick" Procopio and Juan Soto, and others, but of all the badmen who roamed the West, Dick Fellows was certainly one of the most amazing. He tried hard to be a real "bad-man," but somehow he just couldn't do it right! It was all because of his one serious failing. You see, Dick couldn't ride a horse. He could sit in a saddle all right, but never for very long. It's pretty hard to be a successful stagecoach robber when you can't ride away!

In 1869 Dick was caught trying to rob a stage near Los Angeles and was sentenced to prison. He was a good prisoner, so good that he was given a pardon in 1874. For almost two years Dick behaved himself, but that was too good to last.

Our adventure with Dick opens as Wells, Fargo was shipping gold worth $240,000 to Los Angeles. The well guarded gold bricks were to go by Southern Pacific as far as the train tracks went, then by stage-coach for the rest of the trip. Those two Wells, Fargo detectives, Sam Brastow and J. B. Hume were on hand, as well as a chief of police and several other guards. Watching the heavy boxes move from train to stage was our friend Dick.

His plans were simple. He'd ride across the country, stop the coach on a steep hill and take the gold. What could be easier? First however, he very properly rented a horse from the local livery stable and rode off. Within half an hour of being ridden out of town by Dick, the horse returned, alone! Shortly after, Dick limped back, some-what sadder. By now he had missed the morning stage and the heavy treasure boxes. But—there was an evening stage and it too carried an express box, so he still had another chance.

This time he stole a horse, rode out of town and hid to wait for the evening stage. When it arrived the driver quickly threw down the box at Dick's gruff command and rattled on down the road. Dick had no way of opening the box, so he had to take it with him, but this horse had other ideas too. When he saw Dick coming towards him with the heavy box, he tossed his head and ran.

But Dick wasn't through yet! He picked up the treasure and slowly made his way up over the hill. He knew a railroad work camp was close by, where he hoped to find the tools to open his box. On the other side of the hill Dick found what he was looking for. He also found an 18-foot air shaft, dropped into it, and broke his leg. Crawling and dragging the box from the shaft to the end of the tunnel, he opened the box with an ax. His loot was $1800. From the branches of a nearby tree he cut crutches and with the money in hand, hobbled off towards the nearest ranch, for he wanted—a horse!

He found three horses, all newly shod. One animal, however, had been fitted with an odd shoe, a mule shoe. This was the horse Dick picked. With such a clear track to follow, it was no trouble for the sheriff and Wells, Fargo men to capture Dick. Before he could be taken to prison, however, he escaped. Now that isn't an easy trick for a man on crutches, but Dick made it. He stumped several miles to another ranch where he again stole a horse. This animal, like all the rest, ran when he saw Dick hobbling toward him dragging a saddle. It seems that seeing Dick Fellows was just too much for any good animal to take.

After five years in jail, this almost-successful bandit committed several more stage robberies. Then, while Dick was being held in the Santa Barbara jail, he escaped again and found, tied close by, a fine looking horse, which he promptly took. With a rope looped over the animal's head as a bridle, Dick mounted, dug his heels in, and away they went! For about two hundred yards, that is, for suddenly the horse stopped, and went wild. Early morning risers were given quite a show as the animal bucked, twisted, turned and finally bounced the daring Dick Fellows off. There were no more escapes for him after that, and what is even better, no more horses either.

Amid all the western stories of brave, handsome bandits, the real

It was no trouble to capture Dick

story of Black Bart is an unusual one. Bart was a skinny little fellow, bald and short, who wrote bad poetry and didn't own a horse. He walked to and away from his crimes. His shotgun was so rusty that it wouldn't have fired even if he had wanted it to. Black Bart covered his head with a flour sack, cutting two holes in it so that he might see. Yet this quiet little man was the most successful bandit in the history of the West. He robbed 28 stages, all the while working alone.

In 1875 Black Bart stopped his first stage. Well, stopped is hardly the word for it. The driver, unarmed as he was, was so surprised to see the strange figure with the deep voice who appeared in the road, that he threw down the box, whipped up the team, and kept going. Bart made about a thousand dollars in that robbery. For the next eight years he would suddenly appear every three or four months in front of some un-suspecting stage driver, would hold up the stage, then disappear. His costume was always the same—linen duster, shotgun, and flour-sack mask.

Wells, Fargo detective Hume was anxious to get Black Bart. No bandit in Wells, Fargo history had been more successful. He must be stopped.

His twenty-eighth holdup was his last. Between Sonora and Copper-opolis on a November morning in 1883, Reason McConnell was driving stage for the Nevada Stage Company. Just to make it hard for fellows like Black Bart, the express box had been bolted to the floor of the coach, inside under a seat. With McConnell was his young friend, Jimmy Rolleri. Jimmy had just received a new rifle and was going to do a little rabbit hunting with it.

At the bottom of Funk's hill, Jimmy got out of the stage, planning to hunt his way around the hill and meet the stage on the other side. McConnell drove on, but at the top of the hill, Black Bart stepped out and ordered the driver to "Throw down the box!" Reason McConnell could not do this, as he explained to the masked man. Bart then ordered him down from the stage, told him to unhitch the team, drive them over the top of the hill and stay there. Quickly Bart worked on the box, but in all his robberies he'd never taken so long.

Meanwhile, over the hill, McConnell hadn't just been sitting. He got

Jimmy's attention quietly, for Jimmy had the only gun between them. The two moved up to the top of the hill just as Bart was backing out of the stage with his loot. Jim's new rifle fired away, not just once but three times. It's never been decided who fired those shots, but all except one missed. The last shot clipped the bandit's clothes.

Wells, Fargo Detective Hume quickly arrived in San Andreas to go over the evidence found at the scene. He found a neat black derby, magnifying glasses, field glasses, and a handkerchief. In one corner of the handkerchief was a laundry mark, and that mark was the clue Hume used to find the criminal.

He checked with ninety-one San Francisco laundries, and learned that the mark found on Bart's handkerchief was also the mark placed on the laundry of one C. E. Bolton. Now Mr. Bolton was a most respectable man, a wealthy gentleman with mining interests in the hills. He often took long trips into the mining country, but always returned to his home, which was, by the way, across from one of San Francisco's police stations. In fact, Mr. Bolton often ate with the gentlemen of the police department and was quite interested in the bandit Black Bart.

here I lay me down to sleep
to wait the coming morrow
perhaps Success perhaps defeat
And everlasting Sorrow
let come what will I'll try it on
my condition cant be worse
and if theres money in that Box
Tis munny in my purse
Black Bart
the Po8

Carefully Detective Hume questioned Mr. Bolton, then filed an official report which read:

Bolton, Charles E., alias C. E. Bolton, alias Black Bart, the PO-8, age 55 years; Occupation, miner; Height 5 ft. 7½ inches; Color of hair, gray; color of eyes, blue; gunshot wound on side. He is well educated, well informed man, has few friends. He is a remarkable walker, has great strength, endurance.

Black Bart (or C. E. Bolton) pleaded guilty to that one crime of robbing McConnell's stage. He received a six-year sentence and after release from prison, he vanished!

Other road agents reached their end behind bars or by way of the rope. The growth of stage service in Oregon and Washington brought robberies like those in California. In 1868 Wyoming, Idaho, and Montana had mining booms. Miners who followed the booms were followed by expressmen, shopkeepers, stagemen, and by rowdy badmen, too.

These new territories were far from the United States government in Washington, D.C. Because of this, outlaws of all kinds became familiar figures in many towns. Finally groups of citizens took the law into their own hands, and ended the careers of many western badmen. These groups were called Vigilantes. They often took action only when they were very angry, so they did make mistakes. Without them, however, there would have been even less law and order, for the government took little interest in the vast unsettled West at this time.

In Virginia City, Montana, there was a regular crime wave. The sheriff, one Henry Plummer, couldn't seem to solve the crimes. Almost a year later the citizens of Virginia City learned why. The sheriff himself was the leader of about a hundred outlaws. Vigilantes hanged the sheriff and several of his pals. Between 1863 and 1866 thirty-two road agents died at the hands of Montana Vigilantes.

It is said that no man in the United States ever handled more money in gold dust and coins than did Pilsbury "Chips" Hodkins. Chips was an express messenger in the western states for over twenty-five years. He was never held up, never lost a shipment, and never traveled armed.

Chips proved that he could outwit would-be robbers. On one trip he became suspicious of two fellows with bad reputations who asked too many questions. His express bags included an extra heavy shipment of gold. Leaving town as usual, Chips turned off the main trail, hid in the brush, and waited. Sure enough, two hard-running horses were close behind him. He could hear the riders talking as they galloped past over the hill. "If we don't catch him on this hill, we will on the next," they said.

Riding quickly around the bottom of that hill, Chips took every short-cut he knew to get to the next town. He had already delivered the express and was on his way before the would-be robbers arrived and learned they had been outsmarted. Many months later Chips met the two men again. They boldly winked at him and said, "Chips, you sure know your business!" That he did!

Vigilante justice was fast and final

When Wells, Fargo bought Reynolds & Todd Express in 1853, they got Chips along with the business. It was a deal they never were to feel sorry about. When Chips retired after long service to the company, President Henry Wells gave a huge party in his honor. Over five hundred people were invited and many speeches were made telling of this pioneer expressman's loyal work. Chips was so thrilled with all the honors and with the beautiful gifts that he hardly knew what to say. Finally he found the words: "I only did my duty."

Peace Officers led respectable lives. They were admired, well liked, and looked up to in their communities. Like Chips Hodkins, they "only did their duty!" However, they proved the simple slogan that Bandit Dick Fellows wrote before entering prison for his final stay. "Crime," Dick wrote, "It don't pay!" It was the guards, detectives, and shotgun messengers who made it so.

They built 165 stage stations in a year

THE LONGEST STAGECOACH RIDE EVER!

Today we cross the great wall of mountains, the hot desert, and the three thousand miles that separate our western states from the East with little thought of the travel problems the pioneer faced. In fast sailing ships, with good crews and able seamen, and the best weather, it still took a hundred and ninety days to get to California around the tip of Cape Horn. It was much faster to cross the Isthmus of Panama, but even that took two months! There was also the danger of yellow fever which killed thousands of the Panama travelers. Crossing the United States by land was cheaper, some travelers said. There was only the fear of Indians, of dying of hunger or thirst, or getting lost in the vast unmapped land to worry about.

It is unlikely that any man in the West knew of the need for overland stage service better than Jim Birch, President of the California Stage Company. After 1851, he would often leave his wife and baby in their beautiful new mansion in Massachusetts, to make regular trips to San Francisco by steamship. Traveling this route as often as he did proved to Jim how much the West needed overland service. Furthermore, who would be better able to provide it than the California Stage Company? Talking the whole matter over with his Vice President, Frank Stevens, and others in the company, Jim decided to try to get a government mail contract and open the overland route.

It was August 20, 1857 when Jim Birch said goodby to Frank, to the stage line he had built, and to California. It was to be his last trip. He never had a chance to get the overland contract, for, not many days later, the steamship *Central America,* carrying Jim and thirty-nine others, sank in a fierce Atlantic storm. Jim Birch was dead. His lifelong friend and pal, Frank Stevens, must now run the stage lines Jim had

OVERLAND STAGE ROUTES FROM THE MISSISSIPPI TO THE WEST

GREAT

PLAINS

UNION PACIFIC R.R.

LEAVENWORTH & PIKES PEAK

PLATTE RIVER ROUTE

LEAVENWORTH & PIKES PEAK EXPRESS CO

SANTE FE MAIL

BUTTERFIELD'S SOUTHERN OVERLAND ROUTE

CHICAGO

OMAHA

ST. JOSEPH

DENVER

INDEPENDENCE

TIPTON

ST. LOUIS

FT. LARNED

started. Stages of the California Stage Company pushed on over the Sierra in regular runs. Birch's stages were the first to cross the southern lands from Texas to San Diego, California. The little mission city of San Diego went wild with joy when those first jackass-drawn mail coaches arrived, but Jim Birch wasn't there.

The honor of planning the first overland passenger and mail service fell to another Easterner named John Butterfield. He was quite a businessman and finally was one of the leading expressmen in the country. In the East he was in business with William Fargo, and was a friend of President Buchanan. With Fargo and others, Butterfield formed the *Great Overland Mail Company*. This firm received the government contract to deliver mail to the West.

They were given just one year to get their stages on the road. One year, and in that time they had to build 165 stations across the southern

The crowd shrieked and whistled—the Overland Stage had arrived!

part of the country. These were to be made of adobe, stone, or logs. There were 165 wells to dig for as many corrals; tanks and tank wagons to be built, bridges to construct, blacksmith shops and repair shops to set up and supply. There were three thousand miles of road. At certain stations there would be some twelve hundred horses, six hundred mules, hay and grain by the thousands of tons, and a hundred stage wagons and coaches. Besides all this, there were men to hire, over seven hundred and fifty of them. The job seemed almost impossible, but it wasn't! On the very day the stages were due to roll, according to contract, roll they did!

On September 15, 1858, the first coaches started their trip. Some stations weren't built, others were unfinished. Butterfield had agreed to carry the mail between San Francisco and St. Louis, Missouri, and Memphis, Tennessee twice a week. The trip was to take twenty-five days, but experts said it couldn't be done in less than thirty-five, maybe even

forty days. Both the East- and West-bound stages arrived not only within the time, but in less than twenty-four days.

It was a sight to remember, the day the coach first came into San Francisco. Flags were hung from windows and rooftops. Cannons and a brass band boomed their welcome. The crowd yelled and shrieked and whistled! Hats were tossed into the air and fell under a thousand stamping feet. The coach itself, drawn by six sweating gray horses, came rattling through the streets. The driver sat tall on his box, nodding at times to the wild, happy crowd. The overland stage had arrived!

Six hundred Comanches stopped the stage

As the weeks and months passed and the stages continued their regular trips, one could hear the word "Overland" on every tongue. You could buy "overland hats," "overland boots," and "overland coats." What stage man could have been prouder than John Butterfield?

Even in Indian country he was given attention. The Cherokee Indians called him the "Great Father of the Swift Wagon."

It was an amazing thing to Indians on the plains. At one time some six hundred Comanches stopped the stage and made the driver and passengers wait for over five hours while they carefully inspected this strange vehicle. They looked under the seats, unstrapped the boots, looked at the wheels, the mail sacks, the thoroughbraces. Then at last they let the wagon go with final instructions to the driver, "You go! Go swift!"

By the end of 1860 Butterfield was having Indian problems all along his line. Stages needed stations, stage stations had horses, and Indians

often needed horses. It was very simple. Butterfield was allowed to run his swift wagons across Indian land. They in turn would help themselves to Butterfield's stock.

Apache Indian uprisings brought other dangers to the stage. Many tales are told of brave, armed passengers and drivers who fought it out with revolvers and rifles against Indian arrows and bullets. In spite of these problems, the overland stage came through, covering the distance in twenty-four days, then in twenty-three, and even twenty-one. Later, with a shorter route, the stages made the crossing in seventeen days.

For the next three years Butterfield Overland Mail stages raced over trails marked by the earlier pioneers. Usually passengers were few. The trip cost $200, and besides, there was the thought of sitting for three weeks in a jolting, rattling, dusty coach. Sleeping was done sitting up, if at all. At various stations along the way the passengers were fed simple foods, sometimes stale or spoiled. Only healthy travelers could stand the trip.

Express business, mail, and extra money from the government made the line pay. There were few passengers willing to travel the route except on business. Besides Butterfield Overland Mail there was Birch's Texas to San Diego "jackass mail," and the Kansas-Stockton Express.

One of the best known stage lines was first a freighting firm. Russell, Majors, and Waddell were very successful freighters on the great plains when Bill Russell talked his partners into starting a stagecoach line from Pike's Peak to Salt Lake City, Utah. Later they ran a pony express of horsemen who carried the mail between Missouri and California in just ten days. Neither their Pony Express or stagecoaches made money for they had no government contract to help cover the expenses. The Pony Express went out of business when the Overland Telegraph Company wires crossed the country. Other business problems forced them to sell the other equipment. Their stage line was sold to Ben Holladay, the man who would rule staging for the next five years.

Ben Holladay was not a staging man. The business into which Russell, Majors and Waddell put their lives was just another business to him. He was already a millionaire when he bought their line, but he wanted to be even richer. He was rough and had little education, but he was a smart businessman.

First he had to put the line on a schedule. Army troops who had helped keep the Indians under control had been called away to fight the Civil War. Indians interrupted Ben Holladay's plans, but not for long, he hoped. To run his lines he hired the toughest men he could find. They didn't have to know much about staging, but they had to know how to shoot. Many of these men were outlaws.

One of Holladay's prize employees was the well known killer, Joseph A. Slade. This man, who had killed more than twenty-six people, was placed in charge of a division and given the title Division Agent. He was heartless. Once a storekeeper near Slade's station said some things about him which were true, but which Slade didn't like. Slade called on the man and ordered a drink. When the merchant turned his back to get it, Slade killed him. The man's wife began running, her child held tightly in her arms. Slade killed them both, along with three or four witnesses, before going back to attend to Ben Holladay's stage business.

Although men like Slade weren't the only kind of men Holladay hired, they soon gave the line a bad reputation. There were others almost as bad, and passengers told of these tough outlaws when their trip was over. Soon the line became well-known for hiring cut-throats, and crooks. It was noted for poor service, bad stage stops, and terrible food. Its mail delivery was almost the slowest in the West. Hundreds of letters were scattered on the plains by raiding Indians or by the outlaws that ran the line. Troops might have settled the trouble, but they weren't there. Finally Holladay changed the route to avoid the Indians. He restocked the line, bought a few good coaches, improved the food and the service, and hired more respectable men. This helped for a while, but in 1864 more serious Indian troubles were just beginning. Emigrant wagons were being cut off, settlers raided, and the stage service had to stop for weeks at a time. Mail was finally rerouted by steamships to travel the long way to the West, which at least was safe from Indian attack. Mining camps were now booming in Idaho, Montana and Colorado. Holladay sent stages there as fast as the coaches, stock, and handlers could go. Ben

Holladay's line was the biggest in the West owned by just one man, but it wasn't the business for him. In 1866 he sold out to Wells Fargo.

The Westerner's dream of overland train service was quickly coming true. Steel rails would soon follow the wheel tracks of the stage. A young engineer named Theodore Judah had long dreamed of building a railroad over the Sierra and crossing the great plains. He convinced four other men to invest in his dream. They formed a new business called the Central Pacific Railroad of California.

With crews of Chinese workers to carve a pathway for the great iron horse, the Central Pacific began. Supplies had to come around the Horn on sailing ships, then be freighted up into the rugged, snow-capped Sierra. Working mostly with simple hand tools and a new invention like dynamite, the sturdy Chinese dug and clawed mountains of rock and dirt out of the way. In 1867 they crossed the top of the mountains with their rails, and started down the easier eastern slope. In May 1869 Irish crews of the Union Pacific and Chinese crews of the Central Pacific watched as important officials drove a golden spike and the tracks were joined.

When the sounds of the hammer died away, the thrilling days of the overland stage died too. Gone were the long, rocking, jolting, swaying rides. Gone were cold meals, endless days sitting up to sleep while the coach whirled on through choking dust. Now the great Iron Horse had come to finish what the stage had started. The stage must go elsewhere.

Gone too were Jim Birch, Frank Stevens, Phineas Banning, Jared Crandall, John Butterfield, but the stagecoach wasn't finished. Some historians say it was, but don't you believe it! Other gallant whips were there to keep the old coach rolling, for the stage still had important work to do. Now the stage must meet and serve the iron horse.

4-SEAT CONCORD

THE STAGE MEETS THE IRON HORSE

The train had indeed crossed the country. It puffed into the depot at Sacramento with great clouds of smoke coming from its smoke stack and the bell clanging loudly. The shiny ribbons of steel stopped in Sacramento, so for a while, the great Iron Horse had to stop too. Soon steel tracks spread over the hills and valleys of the West. They would go north to Oregon and Washington, south to the still sleepy mission towns of Los Angeles and San Diego, and cross the deserts of Arizona and New Mexico. Until then however, the stage would still meet the train. It would be the stage that carried passengers from the train stops and depots all over the West to the little towns where the train didn't go.

Almost three years before the train tracks joined the country at Promontory Point, Utah, Wells, Fargo & Company had been looking ahead. Holladay and the Butterfield Stage Line owners thought the train might put them out of business. They were happy to sell to Wells, Fargo, and even thought they had the best part of the deal. But the businessmen in charge of Wells, Fargo & Company weren't foolish.

They could see the day coming when shining rails would cross the country, and they saw something else too. They saw hundreds of emigrants and larger loads of mail, greater shipments of express and freight coming West than ever before. They saw a new day for staging that other Westerners couldn't see. There would be an even greater need for coaches, drivers, stage tenders, and guards and Wells, Fargo would do the job. Until this time the company was known for their express business and banking service. They rented space on whatever way of travel would get there first. Now the Wells, Fargo Stage became a symbol of the West as well known as the horse and saddle or as Colt's revolver.

This story of staging is almost like a play in three acts. Pioneer staging days were first, and the thrilling days of the overland stage were act two. To get ready for the third act Wells, Fargo ordered new stagecoaches from the factory of Abbot-Downing. They ordered the largest single shipment of coaches those New England coach makers had ever turned out—thirty new coaches. All were to be the finest Concords Abbot-Downing could make, all brightly painted in red and hand decorated with gold letters across the top, that said Wells, Fargo & Company.

When they were finished, that shipment of thirty coaches filled fifteen long flat cars and four long box cars on the train. Yes, it was the train that carried the coaches to Omaha and Salt Lake City. It was quite a cargo for a train to carry, $45,000 worth of wonderful Concord Coaches and fine harness.

Wells, Fargo's dream was to come true. Once the trains connected the East and West, the way was opened for settlers. Traveling no more by hard-riding wagons or being chased by Indians, these settlers came West by train. Once-tough, wild mining camps slowly became respectable towns. Cattlemen moved onto the rich grazing lands once roamed by Indians and buffalo in Wyoming, Montana and Idaho. Sheep herders and pioneer farmers followed. The train brought them West, but once there it was the stage they traveled in! Bright red Concords from New England carried cowboys and farmers, mining engineers and skilled miners for the new deep mines. Ranchers and merchants, newspaper

The train brought them West, then the stage took over

writers and actors, singers and showgirls—all rode on the stage! No other way of travel has been as colorful and exciting.

Stage stops no longer were rough, dirty places where tired cooks served cold, stale food. Many inns and stations were very fancy places where excellent cooks prepared fine meals for the stage passengers who wanted such service.

There were great riches in the West at this time. The easy surface mining days were over but larger cargos of gold bullion traveled to the vaults and banks. In Grass Valley and Jackson, in Virginia City and Humboldt, along the Salmon River and in Boise, deep shafts and tunnels were being cut into the earth. Deep mines needed timber and steel, rails and ore cars, tools and supplies. These were brought from the rail lines by freight wagons. The stage carried passengers and light express goods, and gold and silver cargos, and made good profits. Wells, Fargo had indeed made a wise bargain.

Earlier Westerners had been happy even to see their mail, but the new-comers wanted it on time. They complained loudly when the mail took even a month. Imagine that! They didn't consider the time a weary driver spent digging the mail stage out of the mud, mending a broken thorough-brace, or piling brush across a muddy road so the stage wouldn't get stuck. They wanted service and the stage wasn't fast enough.

When did staging in the West stop? That's a very hard question to answer, for in different places it stopped at different times. The lines grew shorter and shorter. By the 1890s western stage lines traveled over only a small part of our land. Staging was close to its end. Some stagelines ran to towns far from train transportation until the auto-mobile put them out of business. Some buses today are still called "stages" from those old days. In Idaho the story is told that the owner of a Boise-Silver City line bought a 4-wheel drive, gasoline-powered truck about 1918 to replace the stage and team. After just one trip over the rough road into and out of Silver City, the truck was sold and the owner went back to horse-drawn stages. Some lines in Washington and British Columbia ran until 1927.

In Jackson, California, a stage went from the National Hotel on Main Street to the train depot until 1917. The train moved closer and closer to Jackson until it reached Martel, just three miles from town. Still the

stage met the train. In the National Hotel in Jackson today, you can see the lovely painting of the Jackson-Ione Stage, the driver, guard, and passengers. The Hotel has been restored as it was in the days when it was a stop for the best coaches on the road.

Many other old towns in the West have monuments and reminders of those days when stage wheels rolled the dusty roads from town to town. These monuments tell about real adventures, thrilling stories that really happened. They are often more exciting to read than any movie could make them. There are even some stages in museums and parks around our country.

This story began with the rickety old wagon Jim Birch drove that summer day in 1849 with a crowd of cheering miners up behind him. It's the story of a marvelous piece of Yankee craftsmanship that made the whole thing possible—the wonderful Concord Coach. It's the story of men like Jim Butterfield who made the rocking, swaying, rolling coach whirl across an untamed land from coast to coast until the mechanical monsters of steam and iron could do the job. Even now the story isn't finished, for it lives on in the few old timers who drove Tall Coaches down to "meet the train." There are those who still say:

"Railroads and automobiles are all very well if a person wants to be rushed through on business…but for comfort and pleasure give me the old stage when the day is fine, and the road is hard…and the horses go to their collars with a will."

Bibliography

Banning, Capt. William and George Hugh, SIX HORSES, Century Co., N.Y. 1939 (Sunset Magazine, 1928)

Bancroft, H. H., CHRONICLES OF THE BUILDERS, S.F. 1891-92

Boggs, Mae Helene Bacon, MY PLAYHOUSE WAS A CONCORD COACH, Oakland 1942

Caughey, John, GOLD IS THE CORNERSTONE, U.C. Press 1948

Chapel, Charles E., GUNS OF THE OLD WEST, Coward-McCann, Inc., N.Y. 1961

Clegg, Charles and Beebe, Lucius, U.S. WEST, SAGA OF WELLS FARGO, E. P. Dutton and Co., N.Y. 1949

Cole, Harry E., STAGECOACH AND TAVERN TALES OF THE OLD NORTH-WEST, Clark Co., Cleveland 1930

Cross, Ralph H., EARLY INNS OF CALIFORNIA, S.F. 1954

Delano, Alonzo, CHIPS OFF THE OLD BLOCK, Grabhorn Press, S.F. 1934

Delano, Alonzo, LIFE ON THE PLAINS, N.Y. 1857

Earle, Alice Morse, STAGECOACH AND TAVERN DAYS, N.Y. 1915

Gallucci, Alfred and Mary, JAMES E. BIRCH, Sacramento Historical Society, 1958

Hafen, LeRoy R., THE OVERLAND MAIL 1849-1869, Cleveland 1926

Harlow, Alvin, OLD WAYBILLS, The Romance of the Express Companies, N.Y. and London 1934

Hunt, Rockwell D. and Ament, William S., OXCART TO AIRPLANE, Los Angeles 1929

Jackson, Joseph H., ANYBODY'S GOLD, Appleton-Century Co. 1941

Martin, Covert, STOCKTON ALBUM THROUGH THE YEARS, 1960

Ormsby, Watterman L. (Wright & Bynum Eds.), BUTTERFIELD OVERLAND, Huntington Library, San Marino, California 1954

Rogers, Fairman, A MANUAL OF COACHING, Lippincott Co., Phila., Pa. and London 1901

Settle, Raymond and Mary, EMPIRE ON WHEELS, Stanford U., 1949

Wilson, Violet, THE COACHING EAR, 2 vol. illus., London 1922

Wiltsee, Ernest A., PIONEER MINER AND PACK MULE EXPRESS, S.F. 1931

Winther, Oscar O., VIA WESTERN EXPRESS AND STAGECOACH, Stanford U. Press 1945

Winther, Oscar O., THE GREAT NORTHWEST, Knopf, N.Y. 1952.

Coy, Owen C., PICTORIAL HISTORY OF CALIFORNIA, U.C. 1929

Horan, James D. and Sann, Paul, PICTORIAL HISTORY OF THE WILD WEST, Crown Pub., N.Y. 1954

Jackson, J. H., GOLD RUSH ALBUM, Scribner's, N.Y. 1949

Lewis, Oscar, CALIFORNIA HERITAGE, Crowell Co., N.Y. 1949

Murphy, Bill, PICTORIAL HISTORY OF CALIFORNIA, Fearon Pub., S.F. 1958

Pennoyer, A. Sheldon, editor, THIS WAS CALIFORNIA, Putnam's, N.Y. 1938

Acknowledgments

Mr. and Mrs. Al Wheeler, Stockton

Mr. and Mrs. Herb Doty, Stockton

Miss Irene Simpson at WELLS FARGO HISTORY ROOM

Mr. Allan Ottley, Mary Paul, et. al., CALIFORNIA STATE LIBRARY

Mr. and Mrs. Babe Garbarini, Amador Ledger, Jackson, California

Bancroft Library

The Simpson Family, Hood, California

Mr. Royal Davenport, Davenport Arms Co., Stockton

Mr. and Mrs. J. L. McPheeters, Stockton

Mr. and Mrs. R. R. Stuart, California Collection, University of the Pacific

Mr. Arthur Swan, University of Pacific Library, Stockton

Mr. Peter Podesta, Old Time Stage Driver, Jackson, California

Mr. Neil Stark, Owner, National Hotel, Jackson, California

Mrs. Mae Helene Bacon Boggs, San Francisco

Miss Helen Mitchell, San Francisco

Mr. Norwood Silsbee, Sacramento

Miss Evanne Wheeler and staff, Amador County Library, Jackson

Mrs. Virginia Struhsaker, Stockton Public Library, Stockton

Mrs. Dorothy Van Thiel, Amador County Museum, Jackson

Mr. and Mrs. Lawrence Keffer, Sutter Creek, California

Mr. Brad Warner, KVIE Channel 6, Sacramento

Mr. John Witherspoon, Channel 6, Sacramento

Mr. H. T. Swinney, Director, Idaho Historical Society, Boise, Idaho

Index.